SOUL AND SOIL

COLLECTION OF POETRY & PROSE

THRINADH SAI

TO

MY MOTHER

SUJATHA

Contents

Contents

Contents

Contents

Contents

Contents

Acknowledgements

I want to thank the one and only man in my life who thought me about humanity and life through his songs and dynamic speeches and he helped me to become a human and to be human. my guru, Sirivennela Sitarama Sastry Garu. and I want to thank my family and friends for always being there for me.

“कर्मण्येवाधिकारस्ते मा फलेषु कदाचन।
मा कर्मफलहेतुर्भूर्मा ते सङ्गोऽस्त्वकर्मणि॥”

Bhagavad Gita, Chapter 2, Verse 47

*"You have a right to perform your prescribed duties, but you are not entitled
to the fruits of your actions. Never consider yourself to be the cause of the
results of your activities, nor be attached to inaction."*

Epigraph

Here is thy footstool and there rest thy feet where live the poorest, and lowliest, and lost.

When I try to bow to thee, my obeisance cannot reach down to the depth where thy feet rest among the poorest, and lowliest, and lost.

Pride can never approach to where thou walkest in the clothes of the humble among the poorest, and lowliest, and lost.

My heart can never find its way to where thou keepest company with the companionless among the poorest, the lowliest, and the lost.

From Gitanjali by Rabindranath Tagore

Preface

create
meaning
in every corner
of your beautiful life

Poems may be quite predictive, acting as subliminal warnings or messages to myself, but I frequently don't realize what I'm saying until years later. Or a prediction comes true and I can't stop it, so it appears to be a form of worthless magic.

As though the poems communicate with me in their own language. And I am a conduit who is completely unaware of its wisdom.

That's why I find poetry, or simply having the lyrics written down, weird. The act of singing elevates and glorifies even the most ordinary words and sentences. A shrine can be made out of anything. The music has its own identity and is larger and more powerful than I am. With more to say, I believe that simply writing anything down and allowing it to be there, on paper, is a very vulnerable thing. As a result, poetry has become more revealing in many ways.

I'm not sure what distinguishes a song from a poem: they've begun to flow into one other at this point.

Prologue

Music is erecting a sparkling ephemeral tower.
So this chosen hour will transport you up in the sun,
wild with birds and flags, and
these brilliant words will
temporarily rouse you from your rest.

The last page was flipped, and the music ceased,
till the windy flags were blown away.
Climb the steps after going through
the gate for a well-attended walk.

Gaze down, look down,
behold My huge magical country,
where the south is love and the north is death,
with the ocean on either side.

No More

1. you

I adore in your heart the hearts I put up for the dead
when they left me one day: in it,
love provides all of its treasures to
those I thought were buried.
What holy loving tears I shed for the deceased,
who now appear to me as people who have left the realm of before,
and when they return,
they seek refuge in your bosom!
You are the mausoleum decked with heart trophies
that encloses my loves:
how many of them fulfilled my aspirations,
With my favors, I give you everything.
You protect my beloved shadows and me,
who is full with you.

2. the sea

Sun, captivated by the beautiful water,
chose a spot above the sea, on a cliff.
The Sun then dropped low to brush her face;
Last brightness dropped,
a lover's fingertips on her massive swell,
tracing her crystal blue with a touch of passion.
A final kiss,
Dark darkness comes quickly with sable and
black lace to carefully cover the one he loves
so well beside the water.
A man stepped to the edge of the cliff and begged for mercy,
for he had come to end his misery.
The sea, while being brutally cold,
continued to cast her spell.
He knew that only her could relieve his pain.
Sun, too, sank into her arms,
enthralled by the waves.

3. he

hWhite winter dressed,

He puts on his coat since he feels cold.

He travels to the mountains,

enters the river, and

The park and the street are both freezing.

You come over the rain screaming,

crying, as well as the wind that blows.

Come on, sun buddy!

On the way, he yells,

However, the sun does not appear since he has fallen asleep.

4. my arms

Have you ever felt,
late at night,
when the shadows reign,
a muffled singing voice and
overwhelming grief that cries?
Didn't you hear the silent and mournful notes that
my dead man's fingers plucked from the
shattered lyre in your virgin's ear?
Didn't you feel a tear of mine fall into your lips
or my snowy handshake your pink one?
Didn't you see a shadow move through the air in your sleep,
or feel a kiss break out strangely in the bedroom?
Well, I swear for your life that
I saw you in my arms, terrified;
that I felt your jasmine and tuberose breath and
your mouth fastened to mine.

5. Hopelessness

Standing in front of the ancient home

A peculiar blend of emotions erupts within me.

Depression, Loneliness, and Hopelessness in my roommate

Strangling arms and leering smiles greet me.

I no longer resist them since they have become a part of me.

So, in this house, in this chamber,

we bear the day's solemn loneliness together.

An unexpected cold sweeps over the room.

Death suffocates me with its terrible breath.

My three buddies prostrate themselves,

increasing the pressure in my bowels.

My throat is filled with bile.

My bones are filled with heavy tiredness.

He's snarling at my name.

I'm having trouble breathing.

Death is all around me, shattering my spirit.

I can hear groans.

It's a weird guttural sound coming from me.

Deep, agonizing blackness envelopes me.

I implore the devil to take me.

Using the open window

A gust of wind blows in.

A sheer curtain is brought to life.

Its soul soars inwardly and upwards, inviting me to dance.

What exactly is this marvel?

A limp, tattered curtain that is worn,

soiled, and feeble possesses vitality.

Reaching for me. Old pals rush to me with tattered thread fingers.

Joy, Hope, and Love

Death's grasp loosens I take a deep breath.

Looking above, I notice an open window.

Boarded with ancient naked wood that has

become rough with age.

Soft shadows now that it's daytime

A winding route that leads to the water

The breeze has a salty tang to it.

A cry from the water may be heard in the distance.

Laughter, seagulls, and waves

Joy inhales into my nostrils.

Leave this location.

Depression cannot keep you down.

I will provide you with little joys.

A refreshing wind on a hot July afternoon

Friends' laughter

A stroll across the garden A book The Sea

Depression is laughing in my ears.

Heartbreak, deceit, poverty,

and sorrow may all be seen through that glass.

Blood will flow from your lips as it chews through your insides.

If you leave this house, you will face pain and sorrow.

Death is waiting to take you home.

An end to the continuous din of the tranquillity of complete nothingness.

Another wind and Hope brighten my eyes.

Colors that are brilliant and lively fill me with warmth.

Leave this place and travel to the sea.

Allow light to flood you and lead you. Opportunities abound.

For joy, love, and forgiveness. for a long and prosperous life

Look at the rainbow on the sea.

Despair comes toward me.

kisses and murmurs on my lips

Light blinds and enslaves you; they will see your secrets plainly.

The disdain is the center of the spotlight.

disgusting revulsion self-hatred.

Love rushes in and wraps itself around me.

Light, new, and empowering

My heart skips a beat with delight.

She walks me to the window, arm in arm.

Yes, there is a lot of grief and suffering.

furthermore, Love

A strong love that transforms and renews. frees

Fill your lungs with sea air by taking deep breaths.

You are profoundly and utterly loved, so go.

6. souls

We graciously accept the gift of light,
but it will not be for our own good.
The more we ignite each other,
the more we shine and spread,
the more we flourish.
Until every spark of friendship flares up,
until joy develops in every heart.
A brilliant light beams into
the depths of our souls.

7. awful life

On one slope,
there is a tethered tree.
The tree grows steadily for that spot all year.
Nobody understands why the tree is tethered,
and even the tree is unsure if it is safe to be tied.
Spring arrives,
everyone goes in search of it.
Summer arrives,
and youngsters seek refuge under the stars.
His specter And couples express their affection for one another.
With his feet on the autumn leaves that had fallen,
He is alone in the winter and remembers the brief seasons.
Then you'll realize it wasn't such an awful life after all.

8. hands

Life plays in the square with the being that I was never,
and here I am,
dancing thought on the rope of my smile,
and everyone says that this happened and it is,
it's happening,
it's happening,
my heart opens the window,
life here I am,
my life,
my only cold blood percolates in the world,
but I want to know,
I'm alive but I don't want to talk about death or
It's strange hands.

9. without

Only you can touch a specific area in my heart,
a place where I can go and feel you close.
Throughout the day,
I think of you,
I see your smile,
I hear your voice,
and you present softly in my thoughts.
It's tough to be apart from someone we love as much as we do,
and without you in my arms,
I can only console myself by carrying you in my heart.

10. seal

You see in me a moment when some withered
leaves hung on pitiful shivering trees,
choirs already in ruins and without a singer,
where the birds once Concerted their laments.
You may see in me the melancholy
daybreak that came from the depths.
When holding death's seal,
the sun exhales its postmortem flare.
The world is paralyzed by the black night.
You see in me the pale fire that
sits on the ashes of my youth,
a yearning to die to the same sun whence it was born,
to the adored warmth of its nurse.
And what you see now makes
you feel even more sorry for the man,
who will soon be nothing more than a memory,
a memory.

11. i miss you as well

Take a glance at the sky.
Remember that I am looking at you from there.
When you're feeling down and lonely,
recall the good moments we had together.
Recognize that I am present.
When no one else is around,
and even if you can't see me,
I constantly join you in your pleasures,
sorrows, and emotions,
just as you must miss me.
I miss you as well.
Success in all of your days,
all of your hours,
and every second.
I'm sorry I didn't say goodbye.

12. Grief

Grief is intense grief, not depression.
Grief is not a psychological condition,
and the sensation of "becoming insane" is natural.
Grief is NOT a phobia;
it is the dread induced by the absence of the
one who is no longer present.
Grief is NOT anxiety,
and the desperation you feel is natural.
Grief is a kind of EMOTIONAL PAIN.
A compassionate heart is required
to listen to a grieving person,
not a bright intellect.

13. a way

It was tripped over by the distracted.
It was employed as a missile by the violent.
It was developed alongside her by the entrepreneur.
It served as a seat for the exhausted farmer.
It was a novelty item.
The difference in all situations is not in the stone,
but in the man.
There is no stumbling block in your way
that you cannot use to your advantage.

14. so

• 18 •

I have a soft spot in my heart for
That only you have access to,
A spot where I can feel your presence.
I think about you throughout the day.
I see your grin, I hear your voice,
and you present affectionately in my thoughts.
The way we love one another makes
it difficult for us to be apart. So,
while I can't hold you in my arms,
I can hold you in my heart.

15. memories

I know that thanking you is insufficient
for everything you have done for me,
and it is impossible to describe
how grateful my heart is to you.
Maybe you believed I didn't appreciate
the love and guidance you provided me.
Now that I'm starting a new chapter in my life,
the love and wisdom
I've gotten have become some of
my fondest memories.

16. safe

I built a palace for you.

But I made it out of sand.

I attempted everything I could to stop the tide,

but the bastions were too weak.

I had designed an Eden for you,

with necessities to see us through,

but the ripening fruits had twisted roots.

And I served you all of them.

Tell the night to keep me safe.

I no longer possess your arms.

I'll swoon and dwell in the moonlight.

Still longing for your enchantments

Tell the night to keep me safe.

June is no longer followed. May

Until the moonbeams, blue,

pull me back to you.

Every day, I'll forget about you.

I imagined a family for you.

With two parts that played one,

yet my truth's downfall merely resulted in goodbyes

I was aware of the stories I'd told.

I desired for you a future brimming with joy and pleasure,

but I left recanting and taking for granted the measure of its worth.

Tell the night to keep me safe.

I no longer swim your gaze; instead,

I stare into space and list the numerous whys.

Tell the darkness to keep me safe till Apollo is old and grey.

I'll forget about you every day until the stars are not mine, but OURS.

I wished for you a loyal mate who would stand alongside you.

Even if it happened,

that man was not ME.

And it crushed my heart in the process.

I promised you'd be happy,

and in some respects, you have been.

Marry a wonderful guy who loves you as he should.

I just wish that had happened to me.

Tell the night to keep me safe.

It no longer obeys my commands.

I've turned into a ghost, just as I dreaded.

And I don't have any tears to shed.

Tell the night to keep me safe.

I'm at a loss for words.

Please restore what's right before I crumble to dust.

And don't forget about you.

Every every day.

Until I'm blown away by the wind.

17. true for you

I love you, it's not difficult for me to say,
it's not a prediction or a reflection,
it's just a notion in my heart's ocean,
an ocean named Odyssey,
a color called True For You,
I don't want to hide that from you like a jewel,
hiding love is a difficult game,
an invisible flame starving for the fame of your name,
and sometimes love can get lost in the playing fields,
My soul can't wait for another lifetime to ignite on yours,
my body can't withstand Eternity's elasticity,
and the gravity of my need for you can't escape the orbit of obsession.
Time will not outflank my love for you, graves & guesses,
epitaphs & epiphanies would only bruise my passion,
a willpower refusing to withstand the anguish of the clock skyscrapers,
the thick heating element of my wanderlust must volatilize now or never,
we really ought to turn winter into spring,
flip silver into gold, make touch our bread, push pink into the red.

18. soul so inseparably

Look...See how long evenings are attracting.
Inauspicious birdsong steadily decreases -
Dark nightfall becomes faint;
Also, right external the creaky little nursery
Door,
Remained inverse the vacant wood
Where the empty limit quietly is standing by,
I stop, while, reverberating discreetly back...
I currently hear...
Far off reverberations of my heavenly youth
Pulling like a Siren upon my ear.
With a sincere ache I go to move,
Before my gazing ought to affront some
Lifelong companions apparition
To appear in vindictive dismay,
Towards the encouraging asylum proffered
By the warm kitchens frail neon light...
That takes away from behind the half-closed
Entryway,
Be that as it may, held - Transfixed!
Brought from shrivel not-where to this one
Little spot - Staid...
As though trapped in a condition of wonderful beauty,
Speaking to the delicate breeze in agreeable
Heavenly affinity:-
Consequently mitigates like charms waves...
Rolling delicately up to over and again break upon

Mysterious banks supporting Nivians lakeshore.
For what be this odd dream
That upon my maturing faculties does so promptly
Enthuse...
Also, to my internal soul so inseparably
Beg?
Ahhh...But this much I might be permitted to
Say,
Before obscurely assembling skies quench
Over frail blazes of the last spluttering
Beam,
Maybe it is our internal voice
That searches out the isolations of
Serenities decision
To observe and record and obediently store.
Those intriguing and transitory minutes
We as a whole also momentarily love.

19. farewell Songs

• 25 •

It's the way the stars shine at night and the dewdrops sparkle.

How the light is mocked by twilight shadows, and how the quiet listens

A voice so clear, so honest comes from the graceful swing of trees

that offer such tender farewell Songs in a June wind

The splendour of such symmetry dazzles the sight.

This optimistic heart draws near to the beauty of such poetry.

Each glorious morning, all love is born in natural calm to live and grow.

20. moonbeams

Sun stream advanced from east to west,
with beams of light, the day is honored.
Like suns pervade, beams radiating through,
my heart actually sparkles with adoration for you.
Sun beams assume that blossoms sprout,
also, swirl all around with sweet fragrance.
Like blossoms shade of red and blue,
my heart actually blossoms with adoration for you.
The enchanted persona of woodland stream
that streams down a mountain's cheek.
Like brooks regurgitate their water through,
my heart actually streams with adoration for you.
From Moon's delicate sparkle, the moonbeams stream,
what's more, light the haziness down underneath.
Like moonbeams fling the gleaming shade,
my heart actually sparkles with adoration for you.
A flame's light sparkles in the evening
as shadows hit the dance floor with quiet pleasure.
Like flares that developed with heat on signal,
my heart actually ignites with affection for you.

Along with you

21. blissful floods

You fantasize of an ocean crashing through your dreams.
I float over unfathomable depths. Oh,
how I want I could plunge beyond your surface,
but I'm afraid of love. I would have demonstrated bravery if I had been brave.
You have my entire pouring heart, no less than blissful floods.
I desire to plunge beneath your surface, seeking new depths.
I'm looking through your eyes for forgotten riches on the ocean floor.
The sun descends like a gold coin, showering this regretful face. I flush
Turn away from the boundless shore in secret thoughts of you.
Seagulls swoop down and catch the light of your grin, breaking the silence.
of the late sky I flush as I turn away from the long shore of sorrow.
My lonely coastline may flood, granting my longing to soak in your caress.
I'm going to break free from my fear and confront a raging river between us.
I'll swim against the tide till I reach your glittering blue ocean.
In the waves of your undiscovered waters, I'd drown.
Glorious would be death in your arms, your unknown waters glorious.

22. orange and red

Drifting down without hardly lifting a finger
Stolen away by the Autumn breeze
Wealthy in tints of orange and red
Arriving in the bloom bed
What used to be humming loaded with life
Presently capitulates to the pruning blade
Gazing up at the withered rose
Another season comes to close
Searching for recollections of this day
Not failing to remember her sensational stay
Lying among the stones and sticks
I'm the one the young lady picks
Hustles home with the one she took
Setting it in her verse book

23. landscape

Smiley faces emerged with inviting
brilliance as the seasons changed, renewing fantasies.
Seeing you there was a fortunate occurrence,
akin to when first eyes met.
Leaves whispered in the breeze of the trees.
There you unraveled what love may imply,
flirting with patterns of dark doodles.
Planting brave dreams in kisses of passion
Floating on air amid the warm breezes.
Falling ocher landscape was inspired by blazing hues.
Stunning artwork with vibrant colors
In the fall reverie, we composed music:
An enticing start to a passionate conclusion
Composed with impassioned lyrics in mind.
The mountain peaks wore snow-white crowns.
Culminating aspirations into pleasurable retreats,
satiating dreams in beautiful environments
As a final farewell, you surrendered your heart to me.
Bringing our perfect love tale to a close.

24. rainbows

• 32 •

Enable me to paint you as if it were a summer day,
amid lush settings where couples frolic.
Cherry Blossom Pink with a Saffron spread,
with oils of Celestial Blue and Carmine Red.
With Lava lips against the mother meadows,
brushing spectrums of bright rainbows.
Sculpting your grin from a vestal expanse,
caressing with hues within the curative canvas.
Allow me to paint you in the image of the generous moon.
Within the regions of the Twilight, where lovers cocoon.
Where the sky shows off their starry evenings, lovers dream of wonderful joys.
Allow me to paint you in a Sky Blue with a hint of Spring Green in the mist.
My image of love in a flowery swirl whirled as the playful flowers danced to the
sun.

25. November day

The single white rose caught the old grounds-keeper's consideration,

He affectionately focused on it, similar to it was his own fantastic little girl,

The roses were very much like loved ones in his eyes,

He gave them brilliant daylight, and a lot of new water.

He had generally established roses in reds, yellows, and pinks,

However, it was the one white rose that he leaned toward most,

The old grounds-keeper respected it's honesty and polish,

A quality that different roses just couldn't brag.

This valuable rose was unadulterated white, as new fallen snow,

Which just a cool, late November day could bring,

It's fragile petals were delicate to the finger's touch,

Like that of a quill, in a heavenly messenger's wing.

The old landscaper was confounded and shocked,

Just this rose sprouted through spring, summer, and fall,

Every one of different roses had wilted months prior,

The ice and chilly climate didn't influence it by any stretch of the imagination.

With a grin, the old grounds-keeper took one final look,

Unconsciously, passing would before long come all of a sudden,

After he had settled down for a rest in his seat,

He drew his final gasp, later on that morning.

His memorial service was hung on the exceptionally following day,

Cherishing words were verbally expressed, as he was let go,

His stupendous little girl drew nearer, with tears in her eyes,

As she set the single white rose upon his chest.

The burial ground was a calm and quiet spot,

Where loved ones assembled to recall,

A delicate snow started to fall upon the coffin cover,

Lighting up the agony on this last day of November.
The old nursery worker's spirit withdrew from this world,
Lead away by an ensemble of holy messengers, on fragile wings,
Then on through the magnificent doors of paradise's nursery,
Where the white rose actually blossoms, in timeless springs.

26. show

You say I'm excessively far,
towards the far side?
It's a peril of my left-handedness,
that I see the rationale in reflection.
Universes lay inside universes
what're more, colors drain character;
Gracious, it very well might be offensive
in the realm of arithmetic
to give a square five sides;
not in my reality,
it's a case with the top open.
Into that case, I pour
my imaginings,
things that no one but I can see
of which, a few people show
their envy;
they blame me for being in reverse,
of not adhering to the guidelines.
In my reality, rules are
shades of dim,
droning
repetitiveness,
my creative mind
doesn't comply.
Nobody lets me know that
a cow can't be purple,
that mists can't talk

or on the other hand that you can't draw the
undetectable domains.
Venture into my guitar and dance,
it's playing itself for you.
I'm a unique, you see
what's more, I travel in
creative mind's zone.

27. 24-hour

Delicate pre-winter downpour.

flowing over splendidly shaded cherry blooms,

delivering a pleasant fragrance of sweet-smelling sexual enhancer

A scent of springtime love blowing in the delicate harvesttime wind

Our two hearts committed to a promise that day

We vowed to fall head over heels again

every day once more

Fall frantically enamored multiple times

each 24-hour turn

As the light, cloudy downpour descended,

it meets our blissful giggling ascending to the mists

Two lovebirds being sanitized,

two spirits presently combined

as a couple

It down-poured delicately that lovely day

The maple and evergreen trees

welcomed us with an of splendid guarantees,

of a steadily developing adoration that would endure forever

We viewed the shades of progress surrounding us,

clasping hands as our lives were changing also

Upon the lifting of her white cloak,

our eyes kissed and our lips looked

for no a larger number of words than two

Indeed I do

After a pregnant delay, we added another

I love you

28. piano

I've never heard the sound of snow or
the crooning brightness of daybreak oboes.
yet heard angels' trumpets sound
as the flakes' chimes become louder
as though they were alabastrine wings.
I've never heard snow before.
when the bow is caressed by the cello strings
the golden height of the dawn
yet heard angels' trumpets sound
a salmon cirrus appearance,
opalite and diaphanous
I've never heard snow fall before.
Afterglow of the piano
the brittle fahrenheit of the sun
yet heard angels' trumpets sound
through the flow of the chorals
'Across the operatic white of winter.
I've never heard snow fall before.
yet heard angels' trumpets sound

29. molten soil

Start with our planet's snowcapped mountains,

where sunbeams transform ice crystals into glittering light jewels.

Witness white clouds drift through the sky over a sea of blue,

or a sunset sun smear red onto marshmallow white puffs.

The equator's jungles produce a belt of brilliant green,

and the deserts' burned sands ripple with changing dunes of tans and creams.

See its deciduous woods turn to evergreens,

as tundra scarred with turquoise lakes give way to stretches of fresh snow.

Watch as volcanoes explode in flames,

releasing plumes of black smoke,

and lava bleeds from open wounds while delivering molten soil.

30. candlelight

On a beautiful night, a ray of magical light appeared.
That beamed down on an orphanage,
where two tiny pumpkins were abandoned.
To be thirsty and hungry, to worry and weep
Would eventually spoil and die
But, at long last, magic's ray hit.
A most brilliant scheme appeared.
When a father and son cut their mouths and
eyes to give them life with a paring knife
Their eyes were black and dead.
Their teeth are out of this world.
The couple was blind and depressed,
so Old Dad created candlelight.
They were no longer despondent since lantern terror was born.

31. silver stars

Upon the breeze protected slope,
the sharp tang of metal and the sting of salt air lay
over a field of crimson poppies, no Flanders Field.
At years fall, fields of assault roll like waves,
in the brutality of winter-slush, stray stones bow,
like the backs of moms, and little girls planting.
Their nails torn, worn out, and dying.
They drain by the moon, and child, upon the fields.
No white crosses mark their passing.
For many years, and harvests of assault, grain and wheat,
little hands, delicate hands, and delicate thighs drain.
They drain little girls and children.
They birth the fields by assent or assault and in the fields
unadorned by silver stars or purple hearts, they squirm.
Today, as May's sun wakes the blood impacted field,
each valuable drop blossoms, a champions soul
affirmation, the poppies yield.

32. vagrant's land

I'm the person who should be elsewhere,
I can't remain in one spot.
The grass is green where I've won't ever be
what's more, never have shown my face.
At the point when I think back on each track
where essentially nothing remains to be captivated
me to get back to where I won't ever long.
You won't see my strides two times.
I've survived the dry season and I've survived the flood,
I've been where the fire's scorched dark.
I've seen the revile where the grasshoppers' more terrible
also, the yields are enduring an onslaught.
I've been set down in a twister town
whenever winds are a crying storm.
In the shearing shed when the business sectors dead
also, the reality looks at skipped over the rail.
I've no decent terms on the vagrant's land
for he's never a man to talk,
what's more, he has no control over his furious soul
at the point when a fretful man doesn't walk.
Assuming there's a list in my exhaust pack
close to an open-air fire I'm content.
He'll attempt to manage I'm a stealing fool
so my experience with him is spent.
I'm the person who should be elsewhere;
each camp is a rainbow's end,
where the main gold that I get to hold

is to wake toward the beginning of the day once more

to bear my heap on the far off-street

for ahead lies my clearness,

that with my charms in the requirement for contributions,

there's a world loaded with a noble cause.

I'm the person who should be elsewhere,

in my pursuit for they know not what,

where time ahead guides the unfortunate dead,

something that I am not.

From one coast to another my possible apparition

will slog o'er the path I made,

which can't be denied is wide

at the point when I rest where my body is laid.

33. total

It's feasible to figure out where
I come from without knowing my name.
I'm a member of the everlasting creation.
My final destination is reunification.
I seek shape to feel the relationship between
the pieces that make up the total,
uncovering the purpose of my soul.
Life, in every form, in any time or place
Has the potential to become aware of its link to
the rest of the world, revealing its distinctive function in existence.
Be grateful for life and your role in it.
Communicate with them from the heart.

34. the wind

Oceana tosses her sequined
petticoats into the beaches,
as though tossing seaweed from the swirling borders.
She's dancing with the wind.
She swings her skirts with each turn.
She turns to cover-up
Her turquoise evening gown
With capes of fog so thick
The soaring gulls Seem to carry
This is her summer train
As she passes faster, faster
Until her laughter Foams upon the waves
And in the early midnight dawns
She turns to cover-up
Her turquoise evening gown
With capes of fog so thick
The soaring gulls Seem to carry
This is her summer train
To quickly change into a dress of silver satin,
bound with trims of frothy
She teases dramatic lightning outbursts as
daylight turns to breezy afternoons.
Leaving behind, threads extended

35. injuries

• 46 •

She strolls peacefully, similar to a lapping wave
suffocated in modesty and overwhelmed with rave
holding dear and tight her actual delights
denying every one of her diamonds and rubies.
Her powers handicapped enthralled
the fire in wouldn't break out and about.
Enticed to follow a murmuring call of destiny
charmed however hesitant to take the snare.
The strings of her heart lost their pitch and tone
the grasp of psyche harming deep down.
Untraceable are the ways very much
unfit to soul unself and climb.
She strolls peacefully, similar to a coasting breeze
intense rising petitions to heaven pushed her to the edge of total collapse
looking for the gifts of effortlessness, harmony and love
if by some stroke of good luck her aggravation she could transcend.
Anonymous magnificence would break up in her belly
Her injuries.. sins she would convey to her burial place.

36. unmindful

Long slim ring of fog in the first part of the day
winds gradually across the cool water, meandering,
interminably,
looking, moving gradually, apparently without reason,
without course, without objective.
It blurs like a phantom into the shadows,
just to return when the separated light winks once again
what's more, its silver layer of translucent breath sparkles in its
tears.
It mirrors the radiance of the desolate world through which it passes,
like an apparition setting out on its mysterious journey,
capriciously
wandering,
the dull water, its home.
Just momentarily does he contact an intermittent soul he experiences
leaving cool clammy kisses on smooth delicate cheeks
looking for the glow he realizes he won't ever have,
the closeness he can never share.
He recollects.
Indeed, each touch, every generosity.
The delicate murmur of the trees as they talk among themselves,
in any case, they don't see him.
They don't feel him as he gradually slips past.
He looks as the fish leap to get their morning supper of lady flies,
unmindful of his presence.
He leaves a piece of himself on every thing that he contacts,
every piece of turf, each grain of sand, the pleasant smelling petals

that leap out from the buds of the morning greatness,
the darlings embracing on the shore.
How he begrudges each.
Anxiously, transparently he gives, asking nothing consequently.
All that he has he gives, all that he is
without assumption he gives, yet,
nobody sees him.
In any case, a snapshot of secret,
he before long turns into the haze that mists the vision,
just a fog to look past.
Nobody shares,
nobody to share.
Continuously alone.
The sun looks eagerly over the draining skyline
sharing traces of the guarantee of another first light.
He is standing by.
The light lights up as the shadows retreat concealing like a kid stows away
timidly behind his mom.
Still he pauses.
The sparkling grin of the sun allures him as
he feels the sprinkle of its warm beams,
filling him.
Restlessly he ventures up into its holding up arms.
How he wishes to feel its touch.
How he wishes to blame him for it, to feel its brilliant shine.
He spins and twists like a tornado flying increasingly high
until the sun's grin starts to disappear.
He realizes he can never arrive at it.
Peering down again he sees himself blurring,
the glow he looks for the harbinger of his unavoidable end.
Such yearning he has.

One final miserable grin he offers,
a brilliance that includes him.
Vanishing like his expectation and want
he watches life
as it stirs before him.

37. me

obscurity come touch me now
what's more, as I bite the dust I sob
my body lies here limp and
cold
I set myself up for timeless
rest
that come to watch me kick the bucket
however at that point they're impeded from
my view
by a god with delicate dark wings
I know he's here to comfort
me
however passing is what he brings
it's odd
it feels like he cherishes me
he strips my garments away
his wings stroke me now as he
holds me
furthermore, we start to influence
he holds me away from plain view
as a mother holds her kid
protecting me as I leave
the mischievous and nature
also, I can capitulate
since now I feel so frail
then, at that point, I see a tear
tumble from his eyes and wet my

Cheek
it's over now he kisses me
he yearns to taste my breath
also, as though he yearned for more
he sucks it from my chest
his lips wait over mine
for he knows when he pulls
away
the fire in me that shouted to
life
won't see one more day
Murkiness come stroke me now
furthermore, as I pass on he sobs
furthermore, now that I feel no more
terrified
he hushes me off to rest

38. art

Friends, remember that there is still beauty.
When the night falls and the shadows fall,
Music, art, and nature provide mild solace.
When there is a lot of sadness and little hope.
Remember, friends: there is still laughing.
When our tears have been choked down,
When the world appears to be desolate
We clench our teeth and confront our worries.
Remember, friends: they haven't stolen anything.
From our hearts, kindness, love, and friendship.
If we can stand up to the hate and rage,
Perhaps we can be the starting point for mending.
We'll get up early the next day.
Even the darkest night brings sunshine.
Consider this the next time you're on the verge of breaking.
As we make our way down the long path to the light.

39. wildfire

Summer's yellow frocked farewells to

Earth's fragrant cultivated spring,

to wildflower bunches

For the Roses and Daffodils to ponder,

organized via reckless contemplation

Desolate wishes from children's magic, arrival:

Dandelion spreads bright joy

Delicate expectancy is braided in water

lilies and long circular routes weaved in Homes of chirping.

Sensitive plume and wing shadows

Waiting through glistening whiplash steam

where ice caves have been destroyed by wildfire

Northerners rush to plan under the southern stars.

Rainy seasons have given way to greener seasons.

Wan, wanting limbs dispersed by November's

capitulation to darkening winter,

sluggish vacillates the pale sun's Swaying whirlwinds night as Wan.

40. hold my hand

assuming I had all the cash that I at any point cared about,

I guess that I could venture to the far corners of the planet;

live in a superior home, purchase creator garments and stuff,

in the event that cash was no article in my life . . .

however, you see cash can't help me,

every day my wellbeing is more sensitive, slipping further away;

and all the cash in the universe won't modify anything,

this is my battle and my everyday reality . . .

the things I give myself are basic,

loosening up music to relieve this fatigued soul;

harmony, quietness and love to facilitate my aggravation,

furthermore, I ask the Lord for acknowledgment . . .

in reflection I attempt to understand the why,

obviously, with cash I could go to an extravagant retreat;

however, a corner in my room is saved for contemplation and unwinding,

what's more, there I have set tranquil things cost very little . . . .

maybe with cash I could get better medications,

be that as it may, no medication will change this young lady's fate;

this I know somewhere down in my entire being,

I have for quite a long time . . .

I ponder my past and life up until this point,

the ways I took or didn't take;

the things I said or didn't say,

might cash at any point have changed my excursion in any capacity . . .

a steaming shower, a comfortable bed, a sweet murmuring feline,

paper and pen so I can compose;

my PC reachable, a stroll in nature paying attention to the birds, a friend or family member to hold my hand . . . .

these are my guilty pleasures and they may not seem like a lot to you,

yet, I feel like the richest individual in this world;

for cash can't purchase satisfaction nor might it at any point purchase life,

all I really want is the extravagance of serenity . . .

''also, that comes from the inside''

Heart Full of Stars

41. chocolate skin

Just ever with you, I love to have and hold
into the circle of your arms, I'll unfurl;
into your blue eyes' hello sparkle, my gold;
just ever with you, I long to become old...
Just ever with you I can compose rhymes all things considered
for you carry my dream from residue to run, to quiet
Just ever with you my being needs to join
as initial step previously followed to our way of iniquity
Just ever with you, tips dance wait to cherry lips
Slow summer hands will wander immense to wonderland
Whence pearl white strip kisses chocolate skin
just ever with you, pulses climbs a limit
Stars and moon might leave the dim skies
however, one gander at the glimmer of your blue eyes
constantly, I see the rising dawn.
Just ever with you, I will jump to lows or levels
for just ever with you, I'll plunge to endlessness.
Supplications request asking favors from Divinity
to tie two hearts and two spirits in sole solidarity.
Careless to whatever is there in humankind

42. right now

Happiness is determined by
how you experience life on the inside,
not by what happens on the outside.
One of the fundamental components of
a happy existence is a healthy propensity
to focus on and accentuate pleasant events
and file them away for frequent recall
while dampening recollections of painful occasions.
Consider a pleasant recollection right now.

43. brain and soul

Soul energy is anything but a straightforward errand.
This is gotten a handle on as a heartfelt loll,
To save one's sound brain and soul,
To your friends and family, yet not a hack.
They put down those favored commitments as rule,
In an exact plan, that is the objective,
Since the desk jockey at this point knew,
I don't excuse the sprouting job.
Spot our bloodline developed and developed,
Whenever our spirits stand, painfully restore,
Our sentiments might become tangled,
With the one, we regard for valid.
Life's task confusions disintegrated,
May only occasionally get a handle on its rate staggered,
What's more, shepherd an accomplice or life partner,
Excessively wide, unhappiness, and somber shaft bobbled.
Despite the fact that, we give up word swears,
To be valued, regarded with complies,
to dispose of one another also,
our exhausting gallivant proceeds.
Our sound bodies are formed well,
that is the reason a large number of us can tell,
In the kind of low residue and grime,
Into the rubbish of spread desire, dull.
Along these lines, inside, there is ideology great,
Staggers is close to the furthest limit of time,
It unveils directly to our viewpoints,

Furthermore, unholy raises in ooze.

Endeavoring to keep up with our fashioned,

Is trying without a brought,

One ought to connect with the other,

Also, quarrels ought to be held as nothing.

Such hesitations might be utter,

In spite of this, your tongue is delicate,

The people who have shown nervousness,

make some unpleasant memories appropriate drift.

Ne'er consider without verification totally,

Or then again to be self centered and insatiable,

Question is an obvious primary place of this,

We judge that malevolent eats, really.

Try not to place your confidence in individuals' fabulousness,

Since he, as well, is made of cerebrum rush,

Have faith in God with your entire being,

He'll see through, stash you on the ritz.

44. stories

there were stories here
outset and age, demise and birth
first kisses in newly established fields
maybe a stable dance
with fiddlers to revive the heart
there were stories here
springs cultivated with prospects
collect and yuletide and yearly procuring
new sheep moving in April knolls
old collies november dreaming by the fire
there were stories here
obligations expected, obligations abandoned
virga rains that never brought help
curse and bug and voracious mouths
vast fights with established life
there were stories here
also, presently this sentinel of neglected dreams
estate lost to uncontrolled recovering
components painting time in fulvous rot
trust and work deserted
there were stories here
in any case, the wheel does not turn anymore
what's more, the accounts rest under forsaken skies
while life
goes on…

45. my tears

For what reason do you say, brutal,

that I don't revere you When I persistently protect your sentiments,

And for your sweet love I'm passing on

Also, for what reason do you take care of my tension, I beg you?

Whom you shame, determined shame,

Whom you affront blind, I outrage unreasonable,

If you blow up with me, I just tend

To beat your displeasure with my tears.

For such a large amount your great my energy is dealt with,

For such a lot of the heart submits to your regulation,

why demise give me and not life?

gracious! I at last get it, selfish lady,

Whoever pays you inadequately,

your affection welcomes,

Whoever blinds you, your adoration abuses.

46. it holds up

presently pause
Presently it isn't needed.
Anticipated. Presently you don't look,
presently you don't contact me.
Presently it is normal.
Presently he thinks, he envisions,
he quiets down. He disregards himself,
he deals with himself, and he pardons himself.
In spite of the fact that it is known,
felt, and seen, presently it is quiet.
Regardless of whether you think,
envision, beg, presently you are quiet.
It isn't looked, it is concocted. It holds up.
Also, it isn't counted.

47. time

After so long,
the exhausting hours appear to be troublesome,
they are metals,
unfortunate conduits of time,
contenders to be killed and neglected,
repositories of secret, of intuitive aversion.
Just something single remaining parts,
steady, of interesting hardness,
similar to the titanium of relentless time:
Give this kid his milk, so he can go along the streets,
and witness the gathering of companions or
kick the bucket while he is strolling.
Along these lines, my woman,
it appears to be that trouble isn't the number of reasonable misfortunes,
yet the powerlessness in some cases to excuse the missing.

48. reef

To the stone nose of fire while being a divine being
The container pays attention to the thunder of
the earth and the thunder of the sky.
The purple stone cavern's profound sprinkles spillover.
The entire seascape of the reasonable morning is shipped off the tide smoke.
Around then, a shadow is projected on the reef,
and the brilliant sacrosanct lamps and
two seagulls hung by the heavenly messengers cross the blue.
Platinum beacon, wipe the whistle of life.

49. Live

Over our head
Stars streamed
A strong pale star
A star that rapidly overflows high up and vanishes,
similar to the second you first mesh a brush that contains a lot of ink
Meanwhile
Failing to remember what we could do was only a new amazement
The night soul that came to fold over the pit after it was lost
There is a grave sound of prosody filling in the trees around evening time
Gracious, how
It will be a star that followed a thick direction
That is to us
Something like a discreetly determined stake
Remain on the ground and live
Live.

50. woods

the sun in the pine woods

May's gentle acacia

Peculiar and Lonely Vanishing Point

flying like a rocket

space kid in a skirt

in mid

not far

Shut your eyes and open your ears

The night I hit the dance floor with the trees in the woods

There are mists overhead and the sound of drums

Shadows cast like him

White powder of butterfly cruising by

The smell of wood that vanishes when it dries

I need to keep in mind however I can't

stunning in a dull cavern

aurora clamor in the air

The length of things to come is equivalent to the length of the past

So don't sit tight for my memory of the space kid

Twisting breezes round the corner

A tambourine hears a basement Horses perpetually spinning along

the edge of the sun A book loaded with questions

Hold up Lodge

grapes

Saturn

Mercury

water drops

51. dancing in the breeze

I have no shame in looking up at the sky till the day I die.
The wind on the leaves was excruciating.
I must adore all the dying things and tread
the road assigned to me with a heart that praises the stars.
Even now, the stars are dancing in the breeze.

52. your loved ones

• 71 •

There will be a struggle in love for as long as the breath of life lasts.
Relationships will form somewhere,
there will be a lack of intimacy somewhere,
praise in life will flow somewhere,
resentment will flow somewhere,
sincere heart prayers will flow somewhere,
and ill-will in sentiments will flow somewhere.
Even international ties will grow somewhere,
and you will receive a stretch from your loved ones.
There will be happiness on the face someplace,
and an ugly wound on the back elsewhere.
As your sentiments have the same consequence as your actions,
you are going forward.
If you maintain a sense of purity in your nature,
you will undoubtedly succeed on the stage life.

53. chew gum

• 72 •

They're just plain, they don't keep
they weep when they're full, and they don't chew gum.
We are open books, not curtains,
and anybody who tells us what to say does not believe us.
It was a prayer that love does not keep less.
Whose agony is gushing, the eyes should also be yours.
We do not harbour hostility, hatred, or
the belief that individuals who hold teachings in
their hearts should keep them hidden.
They are pleased because they recall their souls;
they forget their laziness; and they do not keep their eyes moist.

54. crying at times

• 73 •

How lovely was that childhood, too; each day was a new adventure.

On father's shoulder at times, and on mother's lap at other times.

Then there was the with pals, which was never before a clay game.

Then there was the disappointment of never being able to catch the kite.

It was an excuse to cry without crying at times,

and an excuse to get things done at other times.

To be honest, those were lovely days.

I didn't have to keep anything hidden and could say anything that came to mind.

55. simply walk

by pulsating heart
simply walk
Terrifying shudder branch additionally takes off with the bird
Furthermore, do discharge place
so a bowed branch
like a bowed branch
In thick brambles.
the left twig
I think
The expectation of returning resembles a twig twisted towards the water
in the event that it was past time to return
So in the twig emerging from this expectation of returning
two green leaves
What's more, the blossom sprouts purple or contacts the water,
the twig inclining towards the water.
from the expectation of when
The number of leaves in a bramble and
a green cob from a close by rough fissure
lots of blossoms
trickster covered in the lips of the stone
From the let out of a living grin.
- When the alarm sounds
over the cross
sitting under mango trees
Holding up work ladies additionally mix
the pack starts to open

56. new dreams

Try not to be misdirected by the scale,

O companion, the sea has suffocated great many lives,

maybe you can give harmony for a couple of seconds,

you have perceived this,

which is nectar, sweet toxic substance, shaded water,

which you have acknowledged,

you are the medication of the heart,

You need to consume this way,

what has befallen your childhood, you have left the stone,

heart, Sanam, by changing the way, the headings will become lovely,

recall that main new occasions, new light are forgotten to you,

wipe those darks which are the tale of the past.

The people who must hug the advanced age,

settle down in an intoxicated hug, know new dreams in the eyes,

which are not smothered even areas of strength for by,

those lights have a place with. world excessively insane.

57. spirit

Because of the pandemic's subjection,
heaven on earth appears to be so hostile!
Life is stuck in the quagmire of poverty;
I can't get up with any move!
The difficult path has been travelled.
However, the end of the pandemic is near!
So suffering simply strengthens the spirit;
allowing the soul to have a strong long-term hope!

58. hope!

Because of the pandemic's subjection,
heaven on earth appears to be so hostile!
Life is stuck in the quagmire of poverty;
I can't get up with any move!
The difficult path has been traveled.
However, the end of the pandemic is near!
So suffering simply strengthens the spirit;
allowing the soul to have a strong long-term hope!

59. snatched it

They are many sleepless nights;
I fainted and yelled at midnight.
My mind is diminishing devoted,
and it enhanced my heart pressure
until my sculpture is separating into deeper.
There is no entrance to west from the weakening.
I'm bringing in to surrender snatched it
and I can commiserate with it.
I spared myself.
I wiggled up in an injustice now.
I claim persuasive and gracious, disturbed yet.
And I hoped it never comes back.

60. enhancing

• 79 •

Rose petals swarming down from the slopes,
through the railing of waterfalls,
peaks, inlets and ponds.
The taunts were thus on the crumbling,
secured to an ambush which embodied
the dampening and inhaled fresh spirit into it.
It flourishing, enhancing its
fragrance to all intersections,
yielding path of time to the static lives.

Kind of things

61. my sin

Maybe you kissed me at midnight,

for the amusement of delight.

My face, my eyes are blossoming like sunshine in the twilight,

for what? My Antique, I decide to appreciate.

My lips were moaning to say NO

for this moment. But what can I do,

You're so intimate to me.

My breath gradually grows into a symbol of stifling,

for no reason. But I can hear your breath.

My torso was floating around immortality,

to neglect my Sins But,

my sin is an emblem of lust.

62. fiddle

The dull day sunlight drove in middle,
The clouds settled on damp peddle,
The tree-lined water pool is negligible,
The air fire melted ice-brick metallic fiddle.

63. Cracks

She was solely in the roofless room.
Grasshoppers, socks and cats
are colleagues to her immature loom.
Drifting clouds, shimmering stars,
countless nights are the dim light boom.
Cracks are around her sleepless room.
where her sluggish frame sprawling like a tomb.

64. crystal fences

The survival of modern man's experiences ended
to attend the series written by civilization.
The opinions of the inhabitants survived
like mad writings on the crystal fences.
In this contemporary nature, trials and sacrifices
for a history of autonomy are on the upswing.
The tale of insects for revolutions
prevails in the books.
A few thousand years have passed since
the inauguration of individual reality.
Despite they retire mortal beings as swings,
menacing flexibility in the community, like monsters.
Beasts do not engage in democracy but,
turning from the same crude we argue for emancipation,
yielded blood and sacrifice our bodies.

65. echoing-tinted

The reflections of the glimmers
of luminous emanating from
the quiet dawn sunlight occurring
on the wintry Ganga river
established another field.
next to the river Ganga,
the radiations cross along
the edge of the gates of the
vast echoing-tinted forth
and beam light into the room,
which is furnished with isolation?
The rings of fowl swooping in the sky
belonged to infinite music together
in the enveloping air, waking me up
indeed, as a prison in an inexplicable dream.
That air blended with the fragrance of sandalwood
appearing from above the societies of the gorgeous ladies
submerging in the merging proper responsible in the out,
driving over the river Ganga, made me breathe again.

66. summit

In this forbidden world,
Among the vast cannabis fields,
As a symbol of freedom and equality,
In the summit stalk, a standing flower bloomed.
That's the last remaining flower of the century is the same,
It looks like a sack that encloses with a drawstring.
So please, don't tear the plant from the world of Earth,
It will take a century for it to blossom again.
So, show some compassion on little pity flower,
It blossoms and introduces freedom to the world,
Its fragrance awakens equality in society, so open your eyes,
my friend, we have the last hope left on it.

67. fire

Combined darkness
Paths of bright-beaming light
Where my carcass is collapsing
They overwhelmed me with a monotonous fire.

68. day by day

• 90 •

I have been cruising around forbidden
midnights in the violence of time.
I neglect myself as I know dearer
to the crevasse, day by day.
I am intermingling in the isolation,
yelping excitedly in the holes of the ridges,
Gradually body becomes lifeless
Peering, transmitting to the last flashes,
between the graves Times moves,
but death carries not come yet.

69. here

I can feel mysterious and warm inside
with the inexplicable bliss of satisfaction maybe.
I'm a boy or a girl,
it never affects but I'm pure here.

70. I lose

I can determine particular echoes around me.
I was a little dismayed someone snatched
my skull and attempting heavier to pluck me out from
the bliss of amusement.
I declined to appear out,
but there is no chance it was awkward.
I club in my anticipation and no one serves me at last;
The wrestling concluded he won; I lose.

71. why

I dropped a season
building walls
they assembled there
when they desert
wondering
why
nothing alone

72. dim light

The lagoon was deep in the scans,
there was a smoke above the lake,
there was a glimmer of fairy in the mist,
its dye was golden.
The entertaining of the blossoms was the pastel of the sun,
the flowers were blushing, and the scant buds used to snicker.
The fogs were overbearing,
the swarms were plaguing the dim light,
but the lamps of the mind were bursting.
The moon was encouraging on the pile above,
light was lying in the arms,
They immersed the milk,
They stashed the rose,
They hid it were in the breath,
there-were three earth under the foot,
who could not see everything else,
the guard of the eyelids which was there.

73. open

Awaiting amazement before the glorious night,
I felt that someone would open the gate,
It provoked a fury to concluded lye,
The suffering men are hanging to reach here
and I have arrived at first. But the terms gates not open.

74. human

You have fewer occasion
To live no chance
Further than that,
Live like human now
You will retire to
Heaven But what
I determinants realize
Whether it occurs.

75. ideas

White paper makes me to understand
unknown thoughts,
unwritten poems,
unbelievable ideas
but some distraction making me weaker to take.
I was quarreling with my essential and my courage
to clarify this freaking problem
but you recognize what? I can't.

76. climbing

I buried under the barricades across the sunshine
He was glancing at the amazing
clouds like mirrors on the wall
It's like squatting on it and climbing
But I am perturbed that the reprehensible
sunlight will blaze me
I was flying along with the curl
I sauntered in the obscure
striding into the tail
Gradually the dimmer will lead
absently from the sun
I scrubbed the sunshine
but I can't accomplish anything.

77. who it is

I saw someone in a fragmented mirror
it was not clear to spot out
I deliberately drift forward
to estimate out who it is.

78. city

Hands are empty,
If you would have felt that you would have
reached from the city, thus would have been robbed.
Now every part of stone admits us, age has passed,
all three people accepted to come to the city.
Now the forlorn men were going to injure the men,
they would have done some wounding,
They do not allow us to wriggle,
otherwise, we would leave wherever
we used to fuel new flowers.
I was a gravel of burning basin;
you were a river, and the gold used to quell appetite.
I don't indeed have the time to cry before us,
the traveler must have passed many times,
at least he would have removed the crystals of the road.

79. arrive

It wraps the lines of the hands
and the tenacity is intelligently to argue
the stalks, merely to be followed by
those who talk constantly of luck.
I write it in luck if you
achieve something, all dreams
will be realized one day, but that
the period serves not arrive from squatting.

80. goodness

There is a lot of goodness in loneliness as well,
without talking, it makes you cry,
looks big and big,
because even in loneliness,
there is a lot of goodness
it Matches with itself.
it teaches you how to live life,
it Reminds me of you,
the things that have
been buried resemble him
in the tomb of memories,
because, there is a lot of goodness in loneliness as well.
immerse myself in the thoughts,
it teaches us to trust ourselves,
because there is a lot of goodness in loneliness too.

Me and You

81. sorrow

There is no party, no friend, what is the time
that my heart is not with me
Do not panic, my dear heart
this is a period permanently
you are not a guest either.
Time changes every situation and plight
there is regularly no rain of sorrow
Even the nights of living without your care will come
just accept that there is no rest for you right now
See, at such a time, indeed
before you have spent a lot of time in life.
It is not unimaginable for you to invest this time
For you, you must have realized off
some unfortunate cheerful moments
In the thoughts of the raise
there is not just a situation of sorrow.

82. till today

The fragrance of you was in
my breath when it was,
sweet, oftener than that,
I haven't found it till today,
dear time, you have come,
let there be shadows of dark
thoughts in my life,
let the rays of your love,
shine on me like diamonds,
When you came to me,
except for all of you,
you did not show me even
once your sacrifice,
You became the moon,
when you showed me,
the way in the secrecy,
then, I put God in your forge.

83. squeeze

It's a voice for singing a song
It's not a voice to make a speech,
but an ear to make a song
It's not an ear to miss everything,
it's a finger to gently trace a beloved
earlobe, not a finger to squeeze.
It's just a limb for dancing,
To cling to something
not a hand for holding a knife,
not a knee for holding
Not the heel to trample
It's the skin that makes you feel
the wind on your empty fingers
It's probably both shoulders to catch the petals,
Would be a kiss to kiss
It's kind of like being kissed.
Each one it's probably because it's only used
according to its role without a doubt,
Would be your eyes to see the sunrise
No matter how long this night lasts.

84. Wipe

To the rock nose of fire while being a god
The foxtail millet jar hears the roar of the earth
and the melting of the heavens
The purple rock cave's deep droplets spillover.
I send the whole sea view into the cloudless
morning to the tide smoke
At that time, I cast a shadow on the reef
The golden sacred lantern that the angels bring
Two seagulls cross the blue seagull
then platinum lighthouse Wipe the whistle of life.

85. very little land

The house is built somewhere in the sky,
without the hassle of any classical
design engineer or avant-garde architect.
They build a house without the sound
of a mallet or a concrete mixer.
There are no fences or fences,
there is very little land,
They waste only goods and costs
Enormously over there, it Will be done.
Nothing, an endless night garden.
A tiny, empty, landless house.
Unlicensed and unlicensed,
no roof, no pillars, no steel,
just a sigh of crystal.
Cold, cold, meaningless.
A house-shaped crystal that gathers
innumerably and sighs.
We are building a city with no roads.
It will evaporate with anger.
At the end of despair, fluffy, fluffy,
like a dream a beautiful and illusionary house.

86. roots

A tree is a tree.
Standing alone,
wind and air telling
them the truth
But under the cover of mud
They elongate their roots,
In the invisible depths
they entangle the roots.

87. left me

Old images came to my mind, I dare
the memory that he is cheating on me.
Images of me left me, but
The truth left me and does not return,
Time dissolves, time is running out,
Lost worlds are slowly turning,
Yesterday the elusive is happening now,
Dreams follow quickly.
The thought dried up. The body grows old,
And suddenly one morning,
They shout, they still laugh,
Away like a cloud is the help,
But yesterday I was still young,
In my hands, the light played sweet,
And in my heart nestled love,
Why did spring leave, why tell me how?
And my existence is nailed,
My Thought is stripped naked,
The Light is shattered by my life,
Lost attempt the calculus,
He left yellow in the summer,
Winter bathed me and made me rage,
The strange world surrounds me,
And all effort is a waste.

88. calm

And you without noticing that my eyes scream,
Without even knowing that my hands speak,
That my whole body says that it loves you,
That seeing you brings me tempest and calm.
And what you don't know
That my butterflies, revolted, anxious,
The Escape without light,
Seeking refuge in another abode
That they are your chest, your body, your bed.
And I who get lost with this passion
And you who walk away
Without even noticing that my eyes scream,
that my hands speak,
That My whole body says that it loves you.

89. sign a star

Give me a smile a special look a kiss from your lips
that can make me fall in love,
Give me a whole day that you share with me
so, you can see how much I long to make you happy.
Give me a minute moment of passion to show
you in a kiss how much I love you, my love.
Give me a sign a star by shining arose
that beats and takes me to your home.
and finally, I ask you to give me your heart to love it
and love it and carry it with all my love.

90. loneliness!

You have me in your hands
and you read me the same as a book.
You know what I do not know
and you tell me the things that I don't tell myself.
I learn from you more than me.
You are like an all-time miracle, like pain without a place.
Sometimes If you were not a woman to be my friend.
sometimes I want to talk to you about women that I chase next
You are like forgiveness and I'm like your son.
What friendly eyes do you have when you're with me?
when I sacrifice you to loneliness!
you wait for me in your love until I arrive.;
How distant you make yourself and how absent sweat like your name,
like a fig You are like my home, you are like my death, my love.

91. weak glass

The sun may cloud forever;
the sea may dry up in an instant;
the axis of the earth may break like a weak glass.
Everything will happen!
Death May cover me with its funereal crepe;
but the flame of your love can never go out in me.

92. couldn't

Strange people with their eyes full of other worlds
wanted to sing your charms
for them only of deep mysteries, delusions,
and witchcraft your deep, wild charms.
But they couldn't.
In its formal and lacy chants,
absent from emotion and sincerity,
you fall far away, unattainable,
virgin of deeper contacts.
And they masked you as an ebony sphinx,
sensual lover, Etruscan vase, tropical exoticism,
dementia, attraction, cruelty, animality, magic
and we don't know how many other
flashy and empty words.
In its formal lacy corners, you were all black except you,
And thankfully, I'm glad they left us, of the same blood,
same nerves, flesh, soul, suffering, the unique
and heartfelt glory of singing you with true and radical emotion, the moving
glory of singing you,
all crumpled, molded,
cast in this immense and luminous syllable.

93. ideology

The smell of hatred is the smell of fat meat and
the smell of two rows of ribs.
It Originates from the flat breasts of ideology
and also, from the hirsutism of the class.
I ran into her. A person who hated her all over.
She wore a bleak political weapon with a world
View of sex change. In the past three years,
she was nervous except for culture.
Is this inhuman soul crazy?
Look at the Red Detachment of Women struggling!
She is in an uprising, from the body to the panting
Until they soak the teeth with blind poison
A man who lives only for hatred,
a poor man with burning lungs,
she has come among us,
she has begun to hate mankind.

94. unknown

The wind is ringing in the sky above my head.
One high, one low, with a bit of sorrow
and a bit of unknown.
An old man walked hard by my side,
with his hands and the thick cotton cap on the
top of his head, the wind is ringing, still ringing.
The wind rang in the walls of my eardrum.
One strong, one weak, with solemn, a bit wild.
A child from school ran past me laughing and running,
and a handful of colorful confetti immediately
fluttered in the sky.
The wind is still ringing.
Suddenly, I can't tell my happiness, my black hair,
With the wind blowing, singing with the wind.

95. drum

I will be there, guarding
your tired dreams,
driving away groups of nights,
leaving only the drum and the sun.

96. gut hurts

You also became a human being
You stood like a man
With all that you have
You walk around in all shapes and sizes.
My heart is pounding
When my gut hurts,
Without my hand resting on you
Your stubborn and arrogant heart.
Let your gut come out
When a terrible day comes,
Who punishes you?
Suffering from smallpox.
The days are over
The water
will flow, and
the dead will rest.

97. love to love

I could not replace you with anyone,
not because you were irreplaceable
just because from love to love
there is always a little emptiness.

98. nest

The invisible hand in mine
Caress my face is a spider
I'm walking in the nest.

99. flowers

Reality is part of my character, in the spring,
I accepted the overflowing of the dead,
and the avenues recognized more flowers
and darker burial corteges.
The telephone pew in the rain is like a signal
Time is the rhythm of an island in the viscera.
Open every face on the bench
A long flight accident with eyes looking at night,
When another day was eradicated.
Write all my lunacy,
The bell shook in a bird's head like a murky
and unemployed verse, the city is part of
my scariest part: Show my minor concession
Moldy blue sheepskin cover outside the window.
The sheep's memories are moving hard
My death died in an unstoppable lens,
when two pages of newspapers asked if it was a cemetery,
there was the sea behind the cemetery.

100. story is not over yet

The thunder of the storm sounded across the sky
A flurry of wind came rushing in the manner of snatching away the bushy hair,
if you pull the rim of the cloud and say knife!
Her marriage. The story is not over yet.
The marriage of the smokes with the lightning was closed,
but the elevation is the keystone Couldn't neglect.
If your concluding's accept it and you can see it,
The ribs of the bluffs are throbbing inside
Hundreds of spring water.

Be there for me

101. now

Time has come to mind that occasionally, if time allows,
it will return to the former in the prior,
maybe it is not the moment now,
why does time have these appetites?

102. last magic

That the world will crumble
The system is slow, or it cannot be limited
from suddenly vanishing.
With any love Can't stop humans from perishing
A tornado remains, oh last magic.

103. eyes

Fear Child alone: I used to be horrified when
I started walking out of the house.
Once we would tremble. What a black time it was.
Now the child is no longer a kid.
The lamp is burning.
He is still on the verge of the destiny of the house.
And what they see in the weekly,
what happened in the ghetto?
comes before the eyes.
It is ominous; it looks like a dwelling stuck in
the snatches of darkness.
The kid is no more. Yet terrified.

104. shrimp!

When the winds blow,
when you laugh,
let the bud's bloom!
High above the mountains,
thou pure pearl in the shrimp!
When you talk, my tears fall asleep!
Hopes Are high for you and me.
Look at the doors!
I'm Montespan story.

105. reigns

Have you not felt at night?
when the shadow reigns muffled voice
that sings and an immense sadness that cries?
Didn't you feel in your virgin ear
the silent and tragic notes that my dead man's fingers
pulled from the broken lyre?
Didn't you feel a tear of mine slide into your mouth,
nor did you feel my snow hand clasp yours in pink?
Didn't you see a shadow wander through the air between dreams, nor did your
lips feel a kiss that mysteriously exploded in the bedroom?
Well, I swear by you, my life, that I saw you in my arms, afraid; that I felt your
breath of jasmine and tuberose and
your cheek glued to my mouth. glued to my mouth.

106. ignorant?

If you are an estuary to salinity,
thus, who is the sea?
Or writing on the sand of time,
this wind asks who is ignorant?
Who is running down a cascade of queries,
that stands unrequited. Who is it?

107. who ends

Hear a story and see about it,
felt about it and consider about it
If you are intrigued,
thus, you have to allow these cases and
thus, battle against them.
Whether you have given it to everyone,
you are alone in the same brainwashing;
you are the solely one who ends.
Some people came and described and
those ribbons attached to the heart,
now you break the contract,
I do not know if you can win without those people.
who are yet flat from death After all,
how deep will my heart like this,
burn those memories and burn them.

108. still slow

• 134 •

Sleep, don't, my valuable, the way is still slow.
don't be close to the temptation of the jungle,
don't lose faith Please write the address on
your grip with cool snow water,
or lean on my shoulder to spend the dim light
After the straightforward storm,
we will reach our neighborhood.
They have a circular grassy capacity near the antique.
I will be able, shielding your sleepy dreams,
driving away groups of nights,
leaving only the drum and the sun On
the other side of the hoary,
there are many small waves lurking up there,
collecting trembling tones.

109. cloud

A mandarin duck reading earth roots in the paddy field
And around a specific point, swim away like fog,
accidentally blowing his head a cloud on the water reflection.
It's nothing more than thinking about those is the sun a nihilist?
As soon as I lifted my left foot, I didn't know where to put
my intact body in the fog or outside the fog, as soon as you spread your wings;
the universe rises early morning is a flashing song
spontaneous combustion in the fog If the boundary throws up
and will tie you, tie the wings, you won't be able to fly.

110. water

The calmness of that green cone until you
can find what you can stay in.
Every time I hang my bare feet in the water's
unknown underground flow to the joy of drawing my roots.
I'm not a magnificent tree from the person
who sees us to the feeling of rest?
But my branches and leaves do not respond to breeze like bristles.
Awaken ahead of the morning
a light that makes the roses more than anyone else.
The blue one on the ground spread like a sword of
Reyes, don't think I'm kind the tree does not go.
The tree should be, but it's a ladder where
the heavenly children descend and rise.
Stop by my place and relax.
I will give you a fluffy horse and endless comfort.

111. song can't be seen

I'm not a big fan. The roots are loose in the ground however,
the flow of sap does not slacken,
and it gives off a scent of pain to the pain.
Eventually, the song of the cheeks melted away in
the middle of the night. When unknown,
only that song can't be seen.

112. enemy

As long as this fragrance remained on my soul,
it prevailed with me.
As long as he lingered in my life,
the enemy world remained this particle.
As long as that ritual waited in the splash of the oceans,
everyone remained thirsty in my mind.
Even without you, living like a friend is like a hole
that keeps appearing with fantasies.
Preet Senghor has ever missed her scarcity of black wage.

113. feel

Strange thing is love that whoever has it appears not see it,
then what is the world of dye around it now
Everything trades a lot, the unseen everything is love,
from which the feel catches the same quality in one form,
simply one make endures.

114. wizardry of lovers

There is such uneasiness in the lands of faithfulness,
That which makes the people of love restless like
the fragrance of a maturing,
Like mercury in the hand,
like the most star
The wizardry of lovers lasts at night
In the bureaus of gum,
there is anticipation It is also in the realm
of a traveler of love,
When behavior is cut thick Wearing
the compensations of loyalty,
Picking up the pieces of lethargy,
And that's genuine!
I wrote our lives in each other's names!

115. distance

Come with us some distance,
We will tell the story of the heart.
Don't understand what you see,
He will speak verbally.
When the lips are like flowers,
a cheerful smile will spread.
Slowly in your ears, one thing's for sure.
What do you know about the expression of loyalty?
Confession of faith, you know what.
Bombs will mention others and will tell their own story.
Come with us some distance,
we will tell the story of the heart.

116. perfume

Let's build one night
On the marble of silence.
We are at the head of their wire
Bodies in two candles burn?
When we came down with his feet down,
he couldn't even breathe in the scent of room silk,
Be wrapped like a perfume and in the soft veils of the body
Keep waving like souls!

117. anonymous

We have to be detached at the later stage of any turn,
So, come on Separate your assets here,
Give me all these wounds on my heart,
That you often said, It's all thanks to me.
Then these wounds are mine,
give me a look there will be some dreams here,
Which we visited together they have to be administered
Does it have a satisfying dream give me everything incomplete?
that I still have a habit I have an anonymous
fascination with broken things.

118. will pass

Certainly not now,
Maybe a few more years,
You will be able to read all the signs and
what makes the day look like a disaster
It will become clear to be the right thing to do.
Certainly not now,
It's too much pain
At times there is a tendency to thicken the heart
And you will grow up, time will pass
This darkness is a preparation for light.
Certainly not now,
You can not yet
To see the whole big story
The rain is falling, the ground is wet
The spirits will still arrange everything for the better.
Certainly not now,
Because it's too hard to see
Your windshield is stained with tears and what looks
to you like the end of the world will
become, over the years, a ladder to you.
tonight, too, tough, broken
will crystallize to be another chapter in
the story when all the dots are connected at the end
to this line will happen, maybe tomorrow, but nothing.

119. lower-lower

Someone has given so many beautiful answers to go,
but how strange it is that when a person is able to return,
we will be able to test him effectively,
and the higher the standard, the higher the standard.
And as they lower-lower, we change our standards.
Have I tried more and more times out to go now?
In my old age, I meet every day.

120. realizes

One gradually calms down, grows,
He grows up and stands by his mistakes;
he does not blame them on others and does not seek the culprit.
Accepts his past,
He does not ignore it and allows everything
that has been to remain in the past.
One realizes from one place onwards
that one must rebuild one's future from now on,
but in another way, one realizes that life is a gift,
It is a booty; it is a blessing and
they should not sacrifice it to worthless people,
From one place to another, a person gets better.

Forever

121. unless it is on our lips

Even if it is printed on a blank piece of paper,
we do not have a song unless it is on our lips.
It is lingering in your mind, you will sit and watch,
you will not just sit in the rain of imagination.
We don't have a man unless we take him close.
What will word for word do to them?
How to fill the bottom with water.
We don't have water unless we put our lips on it.
You can get a lot of cunning by doing calculations.
but how do you know why flowers bloom?
We have no flowers except butterflies.
The seed in the soil has only one meaning,
green salvation is obtained only when the bedspreads.
We don't have to grow without getting wet inside.

122. I still go today

Saw a young woman, she looked at me and smiled
I looked at her; she looked at me
I got eye contact; she injured my heart
In the language of the eyes, she muttered something
But I did not understand crazy language.
It was happening every day now,
The distance between her and me was narrowing
Where she first appeared, where I still go today,
I saw that her love was colorful,
The boy was a little familiar,
He was always behind me,
He used to signal to her and she to him,
How expectations were broken,
pink turned black,
No one would forget such a truth.
So young lovers, keep walking in the arena of love,
but see if a beautiful young woman has you,
So, keep looking back for the first time.

123. my mind

Walking tree. why are you worried now?
Wasn't that yours again?
There is no suffering in my tent now,
The color of the flower is white in my mind,
The color of the leaves is your color in my mind.
Isn't it a sin to play with one foot in the retrieve?
There is no need to decorate with a smile don't fill it with flowers.

124. twists

I had looked at the moon on the original moon,
It was the solely rose that was red on your lips,
Your heart was there in me.
The sudden vertical raging twists in my eyes was
the first thing I learned about left-handed love.
The moon was dripping with your disguises on
the unbearable limbs,
You were holding your breath and holding your breath.
The swindle was to have fun,
I saw your shy smiling man,
he had risen from life,
The poison was about to rise.
I had bitten you from my poem.

125. fluctuate

How unpredictable are the two legs?
that walk, one is behind, one is
ahead, the separation is not proud.
I do not ridicule the back.
Because they know that in a
stage this perfect thing will fluctuate.
this is the identity of life,
this is the name of life.

126. blossom

Dreaming of blossoming,
The crazy moon was
Awake all night. He believed that
the bud would blossom.
It was morning.
Why should we be numb as the
peacock dances in the fog?
Why should we be sad?
because the cuckoo sings
beautifully: You don't have to
Compare. Everyone is different.
How did the wounds become fragrant?

127. moonlight

As soon as I took it,
I woke up in the morning and the moon
was shattered with ridicule.
The fragrance of the sky comes to
my hand moonlight near me,
No, I didn't speak.
I Went in silence today
They both wiped their eyes and
walked in a dream
I shielded the moonlight from the window.

128. poppyseed

The mind wanders about
the crops in the vertical shear.
What can I say about the birds of the mind?
Now it was on the ground in the sky
The mind is so much like a poppyseed,
God, how do you feel? How did this happen?
Where did you wake up and have such a dream!

129. punishment

I avoided death
but it was easy to live.
I sat in the dark, my eyes closed with my
Mind is locked. It was easy to see!
No crime, when the punishment
was not meted out, it was easy to escape!
Others wiped my place,
I was at home; it was easy to see!
My breath turned, I finally found out about
The hanging of my life rope. It was easy to die!

130. each other

There's nothing between us now that it's just me and you.
Remember how we used to talk for hours about the most trivial of topics?
All of that has now evaporated from my palms like sand.
There's nothing between us now that it's just me and you.
Remember when you understood what I was saying without me expressing it?
Remember how we used to stay up late just smiling at each other?
Everything is now gone, like water in a drought.
There's nothing between us now, just me and you.

Dear Reader

Thank you for reading my poetry and prose. I hope they have resonated with you. If you enjoyed this poetry book, the best way to show your appreciation is to spread the word. So please take a moment and leave a short review at the retailer's site where you purchased this book. And my first inspirational Self-help book, Death Ceremony, discover it now and let your heart bloom again. Thank you very much for allowing me the privilege to nourish your heart with healing poems. I am grateful beyond words.

About The Book

Soul and Soil is a
collection of poetry and prose about
love,
life,
mankind,
the earth,
nature,
women,
men,
souls,
soil,
and many other topics.
It is divided into seven parts,
each of which serves a distinct purpose,
deals with different suffering,
and cures a particular heartbreak.
Soul and Soil takes readers on
a trip through life's most painful experiences,
finding sweetness in them because
there is sweetness everywhere
if you are ready to search.

About The Writer

Thrinadh Sai is an Indian poet and writer located in Visakhapatnam, Andhra Pradesh. He addresses subjects of love, life, mankind, the earth, nature, women, men, souls, soil, and many more in her poetry and prose. He shares her writing with the world in order to foster gradual healing and forward progression. When he is not composing poems or publishing books, he likes exploring nature and aspires to be a full-time writer someday.